Between Christian Parent and Child

Between Christian Parent and Child

KENNETH O. & ELIZABETH GANGEL

CONTEMPORARY DISCUSSION SERIES

BAKER BOOK HOUSE
Grand Rapids, Mich.

Copyright 1974 by
Baker Book House Company

ISBN: 0-8010-3680-1

First printing, September 1974
Second printing, September 1977

Scripture references are from
The Living Bible, (TLB) © 1971 by
Tyndale House Publishers,
Wheaton, Illinois.

PHOTOLITHOPRINTED BY CUSHING - MALLOY, INC.
ANN ARBOR, MICHIGAN, UNITED STATES OF AMERICA
1977

TO
Jeff and Julie
in whose lives
we want to see
Jesus

Contents

Introduction

Readers familiar with the literature of family life will immediately recognize the resemblance between our title and the famous book by Haim Ginott. The similarity is a deliberate attempt to emphasize the adjective *Christian*. Among the secular texts on parent-child relations, Ginott's may well be the best. Christians will find immense help in its practical suggestions.

But it is a secular treatment of the subject and therefore is, at points, contradictory to the Bible. Our contention is that Christian parents have too often followed the "good advice" of the "Spocks, Landers, and Ginotts" in our society and too rarely invested time to find out what God has to say on the subject.

This little booklet is a discussion prompter, not a manual on child-raising. We hope to be catalytic and motivating, not authoritarian or dogmatic. Be sure to check the more than three hundred scripture verses mentioned throughout the book. It is in God's Word that parents can find the best guidelines for developing happy and wholesome relationships with their children.

Kenneth O. Gangel
Elizabeth Gangel

SECTION
ONE
Age Group
Guidelines

1
Preparing
to Be
Parents

After the music, rice, and lace, a newly married couple finds itself settling down to the realities of making a home. Some of those realities may be harsh, but if the union has been based on a maturing love and mutual commitment to Christ, the early years can be a pleasant learning experience.

Marriage is a state of constant and important relationships. Words like *compatibility, mutuality, affection,* and *partnership* testify to the people-contact ratio of marriage and family living. We might identify at least four levels of relationships—in decreasing order of importance, but increasing complexity. As developmental task psychologists remind us, success at each step is dependent on achievement at the previous level.

11

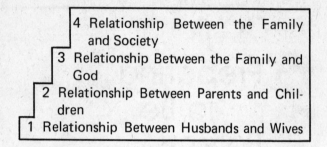

This first chapter is intended to get us thinking together about the first and most important level of family relationship. If husband and wife are not properly functioning toward each other, they can never be adequate parents. The process unfolds in three phases:

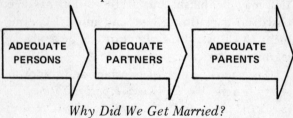

ADEQUATE PERSONS → ADEQUATE PARTNERS → ADEQUATE PARENTS

Why Did We Get Married?

Too often this question haunts the hearts and homes of Christian couples. The clamoring voices of a secular society provide confusion rather than help. Young adults who sincerely want to follow the Bible are distracted by contemporary mores and values. Some sociologists even suggest that the family is no longer a pri-

12

mary social group in Western culture. Certainly permanency in marriage is not considered essential in our society. It is becoming more and more difficult to believe and practice Biblical standards of family living, but only by doing so can Christian couples construct truly happy homes.

Perhaps our biggest deficiency is that we don't really know what the Bible says about marriage and family. We spend too much time with articles in *Reader's Digest* and too little time with God's blueprint for marriage. Here are some sample ideas about marriage synthesized from Scripture. Check the passages to see if you agree:

1. *Genesis 2:18-25*—The primary purpose of marriage is fellowship between a man and a woman.

2. *I Corinthians 6:15-7:5*—Sex in marriage is part of God's plan but sex outside of marriage is serious sin.

3. *Psalm 127:3-5*—God's general pattern for marriage is parenthood and the raising of children.

4. *Romans 7:1-3*—God intends for Christian marriages to be permanent unions.

5. *Ephesians 5:22-33*—Relationships in the Christian home are to be patterned after the relationships of Christ to His church.

Every Christian couple must decide who knows more about marital harmony: God or the sociology departments at our state universities. Cultivating mature love is a full-time and lifetime job. The wedding is merely the beginning and the immature quality of love which we have at that moment must be stabilized and nurtured through the years. Wiese and Steinmetz suggest a simple formula for cultivating mature love: "Communicate + Work + Pray = Mature Love" (*Everything You Need to Know to Stay Married and Like It,* Zondervan, 1972, p. 26).

How Many Children Should We Have?

Answering such a question in the midst of a zero population growth emphasis is confusing. Once again, the only complete picture comes from God's Word. Two ideas balance each other to give us a sane and sensible approach to the issue:

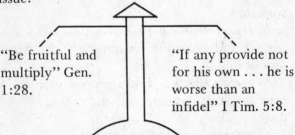

"Be fruitful and multiply" Gen. 1:28.

"If any provide not for his own . . . he is worse than an infidel" I Tim. 5:8.

The normality of having children is kept in check by a recognition of the responsibility of parenthood. Young married couples should ask themselves several searching questions.

Why do we want to have children? How many children will be best for us? How is the Holy Spirit leading us in this matter? When do we want our first child?

Wise Christian parents will think seriously about the number of children. The ideal two-child family for the sake of population control may be based on poor arithmetic says the reputable American Institute of Family Relations, warning that at such a rate we'll soon run short of taxpayers.

How Can We Learn to Relate to Each Other?

In these days of unisex clothing and transexual operations, we are tempted to think that definite roles are no longer identifiable in the home. But this is precisely part of the problem. Even secular studies, such as the research done in the Department of Psychiatry at the University of Pennsylvania, indicate that role breakdown is a serious crisis in today's families.

Talk about love and harmony is a step toward happiness but we can never expect talk to become reality until we commit ourselves to adopting Biblical roles. God has told us a great deal about how different family members should function and Paul offers a simple and brief summary in Colossians 3:18-21 (TLB):

> You wives, submit yourselves to your husbands, for that is what the Lord has planned for you. And you husbands must be loving and kind to your wives and not bitter against them, nor harsh. You children must always obey your fathers and mothers, for that pleases the Lord. Fathers, don't scold your children so much that

they become discouraged and quit trying.
Wives: Be in subjection to your husbands.
Husbands: Love your wives; be patient
with your children.
Children: Obey your parents in everything.

The formula is easy to understand but much
more difficult to implement. None of these commands is popular in our day! Women's liberation
has replaced subjection; recreational sex has
diluted marital love; and the permissive society
has made obedience to parents an anachronism.
Arnold C. Roth well states that too often
even Christian parents have selfish motives in
wanting children:

> The world needs more children who have
> been loved, disciplined and equipped for
> living by self-sacrificing (not self-seeking)
> adults. Parents need children so they can
> bestow their love upon them. Christians
> want to honor God through bringing chil-
> dren to love Him (*The Family in Today's
> Society*, Levi Miller, ed., Herald, 1971, p.
> 87).

What about Birth Control?

Most evangelical theologians and medical
doctors agree that the Bible neither condones
nor condemns contraceptives. Such a silent issue
then becomes a personal one to be decided by
each couple as God leads them. Among the good
reasons for the use of contraceptives are time for
sexual adjustment; protection of the woman's

physical condition; control of potential heredi-
tary diseases; inability to finance another child
in an inflated economy; decision to limit the
family and, in general, a commitment to planned
parenthood.

Parenthood is an enormous responsibility and,
at the same time, a great joy. It requires our best
attention in making sure that the home into
which we bring our children is ready for them
spiritually, emotionally, physically, economi-
cally, and in every other way. Usually, this
means a waiting period of two or three years
before having the first baby. It is possible, of
course, to wait too long. But surely the more
common problem of our society is to have children too early, before the young parents have
fully learned to adjust to each other and to their
new Biblical roles as husband and wife.

SCRIPTURE FOR STUDY

Gen. 2:18-25	Eph. 5:22-33
Ps. 127	Col. 3:18-21
Matt. 19:3-15	I Tim. 5:8
Rom. 7:1-3	Heb. 13:4-6
I Cor. 6:15-7:5	

QUESTIONS FOR DISCUSSION

1. Which characteristics has God designed in
   men and women to make them complemen-
   tary in marriage?
2. Do you think family life is deteriorating in

Western culture? What are some evidences for or against such an idea?

3. Discuss the authors' principles of marriage listed on page 13. Do you agree with them? What others would you add?

4. How can a Christian couple prepare for their first child? What attitudes and habits should be cultivated?

5. We have listed some reasons favoring the use of contraceptives. There are good reasons why some Christian parents choose not to use them. Name some.

2
Getting
a
Good Start

Jack and Jean Whitney are expecting their first baby. Of course, they are eagerly waiting and planning for his arrival. Jean has been fixing up the nursery and Jack has been buying little boy things, but the truth of the matter is that they are not ready for the adjustments which will be necessary when the baby arrives.

Finally the big day arrives and the long wait is over. The doctor proudly announces the birth of a healthy baby boy! After a few days Jack takes Jean and the baby home.

But things are not at all as they had imagined. The baby takes a great deal of Jean's time. He cries all night and sleeps all day. Jack thinks he is being neglected and Jean feels like a prisoner. Their uneasiness creates an atmosphere of tension rather than the loving climate a baby needs during his first crucial months.

A baby learns love, trust, and security from the firm but gentle hands and arms which hold him and minister to his needs. It is important to do all that is needed to satisfy the physical needs of the infant without allowing the entire family schedule to revolve around him.

Whose Responsibility Is He?

Immediately you will say, he is the parents' responsibility and according to the Bible you are exactly right (Eph. 6:4 TLB). Most parents would agree with that premise. However, some are too eager to place the baby with a sitter or in a nursery school as soon as possible so that the wife can go back to her place of employment.

How much is the child's personality formed during these first few years? How important is the environment to his development? Research tells us that the chances for healthy mental development are determined largely during the first six years of a child's life.

Knowing these facts, we as parents should do all that we can to make the home the type of place in which children can learn and grow while feeling secure and loved. They need parents who will help them attain self-respect and self-control.

Sharing the Parental Role

Let's take a closer look at Jean and Jack with their new baby to see how the situation can be changed so that they will be able to develop a healthy, happy atmosphere.

Mother's Role. Because Jean will be with the baby more hours than Jack, she has a greater responsibility to be sure the baby is fed, bathed, changed, and is well and happy. Once these things are done, it is not necessary to jump and run each time the baby cries. That would only condition the baby to cry because he soon learns that crying will bring mother to hold him. And, of course, he likes to be held.

Jean can also make an effort to keep the baby awake during the late afternoon and early evening hours so that Jack will have time to spend with the baby and the baby will be ready to sleep at bedtime. Then husband and wife can have some time together without crying and interruptions from the baby.

Father's Role. Jack's role in these early days is very important too. He can encourage and support Jean by taking the baby for awhile when he gets home from work. This will both relieve Jean and give Jack the opportunity to become acquainted with his son. Jack's spiritual responsibility has taken on a new dimension because now he has a son to teach and train in the things of the Lord. Now parental dedication and spiritual decisions take on significant proportions. They dare not wait until their son is sixteen or even six.

Family Union. As time goes on it will be important to work out some guidelines for the behavior of the child. Jack and Jean will need to discuss and agree on what type of behavior they expect from their child and how they will enforce rules. What type of punishment will they agree upon when the rules are broken?

During these first two years the child will begin to crawl and then to walk. He will discover many things and get into many places he shouldn't be. He will learn to talk and will soon discover how to say an emphatic "No" to assert self-will.

How Important Is the Family Setting?

In the family the child experiences the all-important feeling of security and love. He will begin to understand God's pattern of behavior and parents will see the beginning of the development of the Christian character which God will ultimately complete.

Parents are the instruments God has chosen to use in teaching children about Himself (Deut. 6:4-8). We should not hand over, by default, that most sacred responsibility.

What Should I Be Teaching Him Now?

His first two years are not too early to begin to teach him such things as obedience. After he has been put to bed for the night, if the child comes toddling back with an infectious smile, it is a big mistake to laugh and to say how smart he is to figure out how to crawl out of his crib. If parents really want a young child to stay in bed when he is put there for the night, they must consistently show displeasure and firmness by putting him right back into bed.

The child can also begin to learn respect for his parents and other children. A small child is very cute in his actions and often the center of attention. But we do the child no favor by allowing him to have what he wants, when he wants it. And older children in the family or some of his playmates must not be asked constantly to give in to the baby in order to "keep peace."

The small child's relationship to others will develop and mature as we give him guidance in how to share and how to show kindness, love, and obedience. Dolores Rowen reminds us that "the two-year-old comes with the potential to learn about God, Jesus, the Bible, his church, others, and himself. He can learn simple facts, he can develop attitudes and feelings that will serve as a foundation for his spiritual growth" (*Ways to Help Them Learn, Early Childhood, Birth to Five Years,* Regal Pub., 1972.)

Is Every Child Different?

Every parent who has had more than one child knows that each one is different and cannot be dealt with in the same way. But in spite of the variation, God's commands remain the same. If a child is very strong-willed and difficult to handle, *we dare not back off and give in to avoid conflict.* On the other hand, if the child is very shy and sensitive, we dare not withhold punishment when it is needed just because of his personality. When God says, "If you refuse to discipline your son, it proves you don't love him ..." (Prov. 13:24), He is talking about *all* children. And the process of sound discipline begins during these infancy years.

SCRIPTURE FOR STUDY

Deut. 6:4-8	Luke 1:57-66
I Sam 1:1-2, 11	Eph. 6:1-4
Prov. 13:24	

QUESTIONS FOR DISCUSSION

1. How great is the problem of grandparents "spoiling" small children and what can parents do about it?
2. In what specific ways does a baby "learn love, trust and security" in his home?
3. How can parents mold behavior patterns through discipline (structuring orderly living) during these early years?
4. What do we mean when we say "every child is different?"
5. What should expectant parents do (or not do) in order to get ready to handle a new baby in the home?

3
The
Preschool
Years

"Being punished isn't enjoyable while it is happening—it hurts! But afterwards we can see the result, a quiet growth in grace and character" (Heb. 12:11, TLB).

There is no comparable period of life during which a person learns more and progresses more rapidly than the three years immediately prior to entering school. It is *the* time when parents have their greatest opportunity to determine the values and life-style of their children.

Physical Needs

Our children have many complex needs during these crucial preschool years. Serious parents will face earnestly the issue of nutrition, recognizing that only a healthy child can be a truly happy child. And the Bible makes Christian parents responsible for their children's physical well-being. Paul wrote Timothy, "Anyone who won't care for . . . those living in his own family, has no right to say he is a Christian" (I Tim 5:8, TLB).

There is an obvious link between health and discipline in the home. Preventive measures include orderly eating with special emphasis on mealtime behavior, moderation in between-meal snacks, and the eating of healthy foods. Satisfying physical hunger is a significant part of total training in the Christian home.

Mental Needs

God also expects us to satisfy mental hunger. Preschool children are full of questions provoked by the everyday experiences of life. Some of the questions seem foolish to adults, and their number is endless. If we are careful parent-teachers, however, we will see teachable moments arising out of those questions. The wonderful spirit of inquiry which God has given children is designed to produce learning in the informal and natural setting of the home.

But remember that preschool children have no sense of abstract understanding. They are dependent upon sensory experiences to relay information to the mind. That is why good Sunday school lessons use a fuzzy piece of cotton for a lamb's tail or perfume on the blotter picture of a flower. It also explains why moms and dads should create "make and do" learning opportunities for children in this age bracket— creative story-telling, collection of items from nature, and development of an appreciation for God's world. Remember too, that during the preschool years *it is essential to establish the authority and control of parents as the child's most important teachers—a position we should never surrender until they become adults!*

Emotional Needs

These impressionable years also demonstrate a high level of emotional hunger in the life of a child. Confidence in the love and acceptance of parents is essential to healthy psychological adjustment. Sometimes we think that our "superiority" over our children is maintained only by forcing and arguing with them all of the time. Actually, such a climate of constant friction eats away at the very relationships we want to build.

Of course, inconsistency or careless indulgence is just as harmful. Children must understand the ground rules for the home in which they live, and play the game accordingly. *Discipline is much more than punishment, it is order and system in the home.* When that order is defied or disturbed, punishment must be the result. Love demands a willingness to take the switch in hand when necessary to protect the integrity of the training process.

Preschool children should not be allowed to:
- Defy the commands of parents by words or behavior.
- Interrupt conversations of adults.
- Take the initiative in family decisions without permission (e.g., changing channels on the TV set, refusing to eat food put before them, etc.).
- Combat parental decisions by argument, back-talk, or temper tantrums.

Social Needs

Then there is a social hunger which must be met by conscientious parents. A preschool child who learns to relate to other children will undergo less of a culture shock when he enters school. Having brothers or sisters helps the process of socialization, but he must also learn to be with peers outside of his family. Too many children, even in Christian homes, are allowed to focus inwardly upon themselves. An attitude of selfishness and egotism develops and, once it has solidified, is hard to break.

One family we have heard of always keeps a jar of cookies available to the children in an attempt to teach them to share. The assumption is that the distribution of only one or two cookies to each child at snack time will make them covetous of their own things. But if there are always abundant cookies, they feel free to give to others, confident that they will still have plenty.

Of course, such a plan is self-defeating. In the first place, everything is not so amply available that we can have as much as we wish. Secondly, sharing does not mean giving with assurance that you will not be deprived, but rather giving of that which is yours. How much better to give those children two to four cookies each, asking them to share equally with the friend with whom they happen to be playing at the time.

Spiritual Needs

Finally, it is the privilege of the Christian parent to satisfy the spiritual hunger of the preschool child. The Bible demands just two things of children: honor of and obedience to their parents (Eph. 6:1). If we as parents do not insist on the fulfilling of these simple qualifications, we have sinned against our children and against God.

Teaching and training (making obedient to orders) are both essential ingredients in meeting the child's spiritual needs. We instruct our little ones in the basic truths of God's Word and help them to live orderly lives conditioned by faith, love, obedience, and respect. The entire climate must be one in which these wonderful ingredients are interwoven into a seamless garment of home life.

Parents should begin during these early preschool years to teach how God is a vital part of all of life. The child can soon realize that God has made his furry kitten, the good-smelling flowers, and the cold milk. If parents are quick to make the child aware of things around him, he will be able to realize that all good things come from God. This is just another step toward the ultimate, vital relationship with God which we desire for our children.

SCRIPTURE FOR STUDY

Deut. 6:4-8   Prov. 13:24
I Sam. 1:27   Prov. 22:15
I Sam. 2:29   Eph. 6:1-4

QUESTIONS FOR DISCUSSION

1. Should children at this age be required to eat everything on their plates at mealtime? Why? Why not? What are the exceptions?
2. How can parents create questions in the minds of their children and then make teaching situations from those questions?
3. Does the Bible really suggest physical punishment? How are such verses in Proverbs to be understood?
4. Name some types of family situations which can create insecurity and confusion in a child's life.
5. What about the use of symbols in teaching children (a cross for the gospel, a triangle to represent the trinity, etc.)? Do these help alleviate the problem of abstract ideas? Can they create other kinds of problems?

4
Into the
Cruel
World

Little Jimmy walked up the steps of the schoolhouse. He was wearing his brand new clothes and carrying a shiny new lunch pail. He turned on the top step with a big smile to wave good-bye to mommy and then he entered, for the first time, his new world of chalkboards, books, teachers, and new friends.

Jimmy couldn't see the tears in mother's eyes as she turned to go back home. Mother knew that from now on, life with Jimmy would not be quite the same. He would be spending as many as thirty hours a week away from the family and he would develop a love for his teacher which could become competitive. Soon he would be challenging Mother on occasion by saying, "But my teacher said. . . ."

Although Jimmy is now going to school all

day and his world is expanding rapidly, his parents are still the most important influence in Jimmy's life.

Continuing Importance of Parents

Being a parent involves being willing and capable to fulfill many different roles and responsibilities in the lives of our children. One important role is that of a *servant*. That may not sound very glamorous until we realize that Jesus said, "Whosoever will be chief among you, let him be your servant" (Matt. 20:27).

The opportunities to serve are countless. There are always clothes to be washed, meals to prepare, a bicycle to fix, a bruised knee to care for, or a runny nose to wipe. These responsibilities should never be considered inconveniences but rather an opportunity to share with and care for our children.

Another important role we will continue to have as parents, is that of *leader*. Parents are continually leading their children in one direction or another. We not only give them their physical characteristics but also their attitudes, convictions, and the value system that will form their lives. If we are not in right relation with the Lord, our children will be quick to detect and copy these attitudes.

Perhaps a parent's important role is that of *teacher*. During a child's lifetime he will have many teachers but none will be as important as his own parents. We may get a lot of help from

Sunday school, children's church, school, clubs, and other agencies, but the responsibility for the child's education rests upon the shoulders of his parents.

Sometimes Christian parents are guilty of being concerned only that their children accept Christ as Savior. The secular education is turned over to the state and the Christian training to the church. We must be sure that our children are taught the *entire* Bible "for doctrine, for reproof, for correction, for instruction in righteousness: that the man of God may be perfect, thoroughly furnished unto all good works" (II Tim. 3: 16-17).

Tearing Away the Apron Strings

As the child begins to mature, takes on school and social responsibilities, and becomes more independent, it is important that parents continue to meet certain needs. A secure child will be sure of affection. He will know that he is loved and wanted at home. Parental love will be demonstrated in many small ways. Interest in his school work and extra-curricular activities is important. Dr. Haim Ginott reminds us, "It is desirable that the mother be at home to greet her child upon his return from school." Parents will notice and enjoy the things their children are making, doing, learning, and reading.

The child also needs to have a sense of approval. He will know that he belongs in a family. His life and the way he feels about things are important to the other family members. His successes are noticed and are more important than his failures.

The child's accomplishments are also a reason for praise. When he makes a mistake, he is made aware of the mistake without feeling that he, personally, is no good.

Crucial Learning During Primary Years

The young child is learning many new responsibilities. He is expanding his relationships and must learn how to deal with so many new things. Now he must be able to get along with not only his parents, brothers and sisters, but also school friends, neighborhood friends, and teachers. Christ's teachings tell us much about love, kindness, sharing, tenderness, goodness, meekness, and many other Christian attributes. Godly parents would like to see these attitudes exemplified in their child's life and relationships with other people. How can all this happen? Will children automatically do this because we tell them to, or because they know Jesus said it? Perhaps two areas of home training are most strategic in answering these questions.

The self-concept is a very important fact in the way a child behaves. Psychologist Bruce Narramore says, "All of our behavior is guided by our self-esteem. When a child thinks he is a 'bad' boy, he will probably act that way." Obviously, it is not helpful for parents constantly to criticize, ridicule, and tear down.

Another way parents can help their children to achieve Biblical standards is through discipline. In an orderly home there is acceptable and nonacceptable behavior. When the children are clearly told what the limits are and what will happen if the rules are broken, they can learn to respond accordingly. Of course, parents must be consistent in coming through with the punishment when the limits for acceptable behavior are broken.

There are so many other crucial learnings which are taking place during these years but it is impossible to discuss them all. The academic accomplishments alone are fantastic. Many nonreaders become prolific readers. They are learning math concepts, science, spelling, and manuscript as well as cursive writing.

Helping Our Children Learn Social Behaviors

Very closely tied to the cognitive learning situations which we have discussed are the corresponding social behaviors. Common courtesy does not come automatically to young children. They want their own way immediately. They want people to stop and listen to them whenever they have something to say. Too often they forget to say "thank you," "please" and "excuse me."

If politeness and respect for others are practiced in the home between parent and child, then it will more quickly become the normal reaction in other situations.

A child should have many opportunities for companions of his own age, confidence in his own personality, and ability to make friends and get along well with others. He needs to learn to "give and take," sharing some of his own possessions.

A positive home environment in which trust and love are expressed will be an asset to our children in other situations. The child who knows the feeling of belonging to the family team will be concerned about being a representative of the family in society.

The child who is taught the Biblical teachings of life and behavior at home should be concerned about being a representative of Christ. Our Lord is the ultimate example of social behavior and we do well to encourage our children to walk "even as He walked" (I John 2:6).

SCRIPTURE FOR STUDY

Exod. 2:1-10	Eph. 6:1-4
I Sam. 2:18-21; 3:1-10	I Tim. 5:4
Matt. 20:25-28	II Tim. 3:14-17

QUESTIONS FOR DISCUSSION

1. How can Christian parents be careful not to overshelter a preschool child so that he becomes ready for wider social relationships?
2. In what ways can a Christian parent exert greater control over his child's affairs in a public school?

3. Discuss the mother's servant role in contrast to the contemporary emphasis on the Feminist Movement.
4. What effect can a mother's employment have on the life of a young child?
5. How can a Christian father really establish his leadership in the family, and especially with his young children during these crucial years?

5
Energy
Enthusiasm
and Exploration

Ray and Kay are ten-year-old twins. Mrs. Stevens, their mother, is very frustrated about their behavior patterns. They have always been fairly close as twins and enjoyed each other's company. But now, it seems that Ray thinks all girls are stupid (especially his sister), and Kay thinks all boys are big pests (especially her brother). If they are not fighting about something, they seem to spend their time giggling.

Along with this compatibility problem, there is the problem of neatness. Ray always seems to look like a mess and doesn't care. His room is in shambles! And Kay is not much better. Each room contains evidence of the beginnings of many collections: some rocks, a box of dead insects, stamps and coins stuffed into a drawer.

What is the basic problem in the Stevens' home? The only problem is that there are two very active, normal ten-year-olds living there and Mrs. Stevens must learn to understand them. Are we suggesting that it is inevitable that the children will constantly be fighting and their rooms will be in chaos? No, of course not.

Developing and Accepting Responsibilities

The junior years of childhood are among the most delightful ages. Juniors are full of energy and usually very healthy. They will enter all kinds of activity with enthusiasm and interest, especially exploring and investigating. Juniors have deep feelings of love toward family members and friends even though they may find it difficult to express them. This is especially true of boys. Many times they find it easier to write things or make something for a parent, brother, sister, or friend.

One day our nine-year-old daughter wrote a note to her twelve-year-old brother and said, "I love you, Jeff." At the bottom he wrote, "I love you too," and gave the note back to her. The initial effort was elaborately prepared and probably motivated as an antidote to a little quarrel. The curt response was sincere, but the typical emotionless reply of a junior high boy.

How does knowing all of this help us solve the problems in the home? Mr. and Mrs. Stevens want Ray and Kay to be willing and capable of taking some responsibility for their own actions. They would like to have less fighting, neater rooms, and quick response and obedience to their commands, to say nothing of assuming accountability for school work.

Part of the answers lie in the type of relationship and understanding which existed during the preschool and primary years. If parents can build on a good foundation of respect and consistency, the job will be much easier.

There are many types of control which parents can employ without resorting to anger or nagging. Dr. James Dobson in *Dare to Discipline,* suggests positive reinforcement such as money, gifts, or a special privilege of some kind. Dr. Bruce Narramore's helpful book, *Help! I'm a Parent,* gives many different approaches. One of the suggestions is called natural consequences.

Let's take, for example, Ray's cluttered room. Ray goes into his room to find his library book which is due the next day. Because of the mess, he can't find the book. Instead of mother entering the situation by starting to sort through things while complaining, "If you'd keep your room in order as I've told you to, you'd be able to find things," it would be much better for her to allow Ray to take the responsibility for this situation upon himself. He will soon learn that it is hard to find things in a disorderly room.

If he doesn't find the book, he pays the late fee or the price of the book from his own money. In this way, he is learning a great deal more about responsibility than he would if mother found the book for him or dad gave him the money to pay for the book.

In Colossians 3:17, Paul tells us, ". . . whatsoever ye do in word or deed, do all in the name of the Lord Jesus, giving thanks to God, and the Father by him."

In a Christian family, should we expect childrens' hobbies, interests, collections, and heroes to be different from those of their friends? If they are not, there may be something wrong in our home.

Juniors are eager collectors and hero worshipers. Parents can help channel these interests into meaningful learning experiences. Any study of things from nature will increase your child's appreciation for the God who created them. Buy a book about shells or rocks and then plan a family trip to the beach or the park so that your child can see that you are genuinely interested in his interests.

What about heroes? Too often the heroes are rock singers or TV personalities. Parents can channel the hero craze by supervising closely what is watched on television and what is listened to on radio. Good Christian books (fiction as well as nonfiction) should be made available. Perhaps a certain block of time each week for reading would be in order. *The Family Bible Library* by V. Gilbert Beers portrays in a beautiful way the marvelous Biblical stories.

Again referring to Colossians 3:17, if our families truly *do* and not just *say* that all things

41

in our lives honor Christ, then He will be the most important hero for our children.

Demands of Justice

If there is one thing which parents of a junior child will probably hear over and over again, it is, "That's not fair." Being just in all dealings is very important whether it is a game or the punishment for wrongdoing.

Because of this, it is very important for the parents to discuss (in private) the rules of the house and then be sure all members of the family know and understand what is expected of them and what happens when the rules are broken.

Often at this time children begin to challenge mother's authority and will obey father much more quickly. Here is when dad's leadership is very important. He must reinforce the validity of mother's authority.

It is important that our children realize that we parents are not perfect. We sin and need to ask for forgiveness. And let's not be ashamed to ask our children to forgive us when we act unjustly or are unkind toward them.

SCRIPTURE FOR STUDY

Ps. 37:8   Prov. 22:15
Prov. 3:11, 12   Heb. 12:5-10
Prov. 20:11

QUESTIONS FOR DISCUSSION

1. What are some ways the father can reinforce the mother's authority?
2. How can parents tell the boundary line between normal junior energy and undue rowdiness?
3. In what ways can we encourage children to assume greater responsibility for their own things?
4. Name some positive reinforcers which might be effective in your family.
5. Discuss further Narramore's natural consequences theory.

6
The
Early Teen Years:
Doorway to
Independence

Larry Duncan is thirteen and proud to be a teen-ager. He sees his newly acquired status as a major step toward adulthood and the elusive dream of running his own life. And in our society, he is right. Greater responsibility for one's own affairs has been steadily moving into lower age levels.

But Larry has a problem. Well, really, two problems—Mr. Duncan and Mrs. Duncan. You see, Larry is their only child and in their opinion, he is just growing up too fast. Somehow they can't adjust their thinking about Larry from child to young man. Their relationship with their son is strained lately because of what he thinks are restrictive limits on his life. He is often heard to say to his parents, "Stop treating me like a baby."

Dependence or Independence?

The Duncans tend to think of the passage from dependence to independence as an event. They expect that event to coincide with Larry's graduation from high school. But maturity is not an *event*—it is a *process*. And parents should begin that process early in childhood and bring it to a happy climax (as far as their part is concerned) somewhere in the late teens or early twenties. Perhaps we could diagram the process like this:

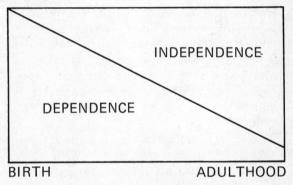

Notice that the diagonal division line does not go all the way down to the base line at adulthood. Infants are absolutely dependent but adults are *not* absolutely independent. We should teach our teen-agers to recognize that independence is always a relative and restricted commodity.

How Much—How Soon?

Every child is an individual although each age level is marked by certain general characteristics.

That leaves parents in need of two kinds of information to facilitate wise decision-making:

1. We need to know about young teens generally.

2. We need to know our own children specifically.

The answers to how much freedom we can give young teens, and how soon it can be given are dependent upon getting good inputs. Here are some suggestions as to what young teens (ages 12-14) are like.

Enthusiasm and energy are directed toward the peer group. Youth activities start at church, and elementary school has been left behind. Learning begins to take on more serious dimensions. Separate classrooms and different teachers for each course are a constant reminder of his advance.

Reasoning processes are taking hold. "Whats" give way to "Whys." With some junior high students the questions are kept in, with others they are openly voiced.

Girls have been maturing much more rapidly than boys and this difference continues until the eighth or ninth grade when the boys begin to catch up.

But Mr. and Mrs. Duncan can only apply this kind of data when they know where Larry fits into his own age-group patterns. And, ironically, how he acts and reacts at thirteen depends to a great extent upon how his parents have treated him for the past thirteen years!

If the home has been a solid spiritual unity during the childhood years, Christian parents have little to fear in extending freedom to their teenagers. Mutual respect and trust rooted in love do not drop from the sky when a child turns thirteen, or sixteen, or twenty-one. They are carefully cultivated throughout the process of helping our children grow from dependence to independence. Freedom is not without discipline and order, but rather closely connected with both, just as it is in society. Nor is such freedom without risk. Not all the teens who are given a wide measure of independence by their parents prove themselves deserving. But parents who want to see their young people become confident and mature Christians will take the risk.

Causes of Conflict

When Larry and his parents start in on one of their frequent arguments, their family doesn't look or sound very Christian. Shouting, angry words, bitterness, and accusations are followed by pouting, hurt feelings, and the absence of visible love. How do these arguments start? And how can they be avoided? Family counseling experts tell us that several key conflict-points show up again and again.

Criticism—Larry's parents repeatedly "hassle" him about his hair, his music, and some of his friends. His response is defensive and reactionary.

Poor Communication—Most of the discussions in the Duncan household deal only with trivial things. Larry's personal problems and feelings have never been shared with his parents.

Disrespect and Disobedience—During his earlier childhood years Larry was not required to submit to his parents' will. Now his strong will is beginning to display itself in rebellion and defiance.

Inadequate Self-Concept—Larry lacks confidence in himself and optimism about his life. Since mom and dad have always made most of the decisions, he never developed an assurance that he can think through issues for himself. Not having responsibilities around the house (mom always did it all), Larry hasn't felt that his role in the family is important.

Defensiveness—Mr. and Mrs. Duncan have heard about the great difficulty of the teen years. They have prepared themselves for turmoil and problems and their expectation tends to create the problems. In an attempt to retain their authoritative roles, they seem hesitant to show respect to Larry. They never apologize when they are wrong, nor do they ask Larry's opinion on important family matters.

Teen-agers need the family. The unity and security of the circle of love offers a sustaining refuge in the difficult changes young teens face. The parental model takes on more meaning during these years as teens can understand something of the decisions mom and dad face and the reasons why things must be run a certain way.

But the relationship must be bathed in love and respect as we assist our kids along the road from dependence to independence.

SCRIPTURE FOR STUDY

Gen. 22:1-19   I Cor. 13
Luke 2:51-52   Eph. 6:1-4
Rom. 12:1-2

QUESTIONS FOR DISCUSSION

1. How can teen-agers be made a real part of family decisions?
2. How should parents meet the problem of peer group influence?
3. If parents of teen-agers have just become Christians, how can they begin the development of a Christian home at this point?
4. How can we help our young teens adjust to the sexual and social changes of these years?
5. Think of the displaced children of the Bible (Joseph, Daniel, Daniel's three friends, Naaman's slave girl), most of whom were children. What do we see in their lives that tells us about their earlier home life?

7
What
Generation
Gap?

An anonymous teen-ager, one of the thousands of runaway young people today, wrote these words back home:

Dear Folks,

Thank you for everything, but I am going to Chicago and try and start some kind of a new life.

You asked me why I did those things and why I gave you so much trouble, and the answer is easy for me to give you, but I am wondering if you will understand.

Remember when I was about six or seven and I used to want you to just listen to me? I remember all the nice things you gave me for Christmas and my birthday and I was really happy with the things—about a week—at the time I got the things, but the rest of the time during the year I really didn't want presents. I just wanted all the

50

time for you to listen to me like I was somebody who felt things too, because I remember even when I was young, I felt things. But you said you were busy.

If anybody asks you where I am, tell them I've gone looking for somebody with time because I've got a lot of things I want to talk about.

Love to all,
Your Son

These are only selected paragraphs from the longer letter but they represent the crucial problem in parent-teen relations today—misunderstanding. The terminology "generation gap" implies that this problem stems from the age difference between parents and their children. No doubt there are aspects of values and goals which do pinpoint varying attitudes between people in their teens and people in their thirties. The world does change and the pressure of the secular peer group will make the teen-agers of Christian parents think differently on some issues.

But there should be two modifying factors which minimize the problems.

(1) The differences should deal with peripheral issues such as music, hair, and clothes.

(2) Effective parents will have built up a communications system throughout all the childhood years which will enable them to keep in touch with their teen-agers during the slump years (thirteen-fifteen).

Obviously then, the greater danger in our

homes is the possibility of a communications gap. And we can actually *cause* a communications gap by either failing to build that relationship of mutual trust for the first twelve or thirteen years, or by acting as though peripheral differences are really crucial to Christian living and family unity and, therefore, worth fighting about.

Developing a Climate of Openness and Sincerity

Parents should be the closest confidants and counselors Christian teen-agers have. Yet it is generally accepted that church youth directors or high school guidance counselors preempt this role for most of our young people.

A recent survey conducted by columnist Jean Adams and published in *Parade,* offers some frightening insights.

- Teens believe they usually lose communication with their parents at age twelve.
- More than 90 percent said they prefer discussing their problems with their peers instead of with parents. Only 41 percent indicated a willingness to discuss serious problems with their fathers (and only 29 percent of the girls).
- Teens believe that most parents are not qualified to help with today's problems.

So much for the problems which many parents already know only too well. How can we cut the distance and span the communication gap? One way has already been mentioned:

begin to build solid mutual trust relationships during the preschool years. Be a listener who can show genuine tolerance toward your teen-ager's peculiar ideas and flexibility to cope with his changing moods. Allow privacy, show respect, and spend time with your teen-ager(s).

And let's remember that a climate of openness does not preclude standards of behavior, discipline, and even punishment. All of these are a part of the love and care that teens want even if they often reject such attention verbally. Parents must allow teens to move from dependence to independence in an orderly fashion but without being constantly hassled.

Building a Proper Self-Concept in Teens

The suicide statistics for the teen-age group are alarming. We are told that over 12 percent of all suicide attempts are made by adolescents and some reputable authorities suggest that teen suicide reports may be 50 percent understated because of a tendency to conceal the facts.

What do the unsuccessful suicide candidates say about why they did it? Here are some sample answers and they all point to family deficiencies:

1. Quarreling parents
2. Conflict with parents, brothers, or sisters
3. Father or mother frequently absent from home
4. Cruelty, rejection, or abandonment by parents

5. Constant moving and changing houses and schools

Invariably these young people have a distorted view of themselves and their surroundings. Frustration turns to despair and attempts to find meaning in alcohol, drugs, or sex. Failing again, suicide seems the only alternative.

In the Christian home, parents can show their young people a depth of love and affection that draws them together to seek answers to life's complexities. Furthermore, they can show how God's will has designed for the indwelling Holy Spirit to produce love, joy, peace, and other spiritual fruit in the lives of believers. These things are just the opposite of the alienation and futility they see around them.

Teaching Christian Values in a Permissive Society

The hymn writer was exactly correct when he penned the rhetorical question, "Is this vile world a friend to grace, to help me on to God?" Of course not. Jesus told us that His followers would be misunderstood and hated by the world. Our goals, values, and life philosophies are opposite and conflicting.

Yet, peer popularity is a driving force in all teen-agers, even those who are committed to Christ. Bucking the crowd is a difficult position but it is one we parents must help our young people to face. Here are some sample issues in which Christian values stand in contrast to the contemporary standards of society:

Biblical chastity versus recreational sex
Biblical eternality versus worldly presentism
Biblical absolutism versus secular relativism
Biblical love versus passionate lust

The answer to premarital sex is not, "You might get pregnant!" but rather, "Sex outside of marriage is sin." The argument against teen-age marriage is not, "You can't afford to get married now—how will you support her?" but rather, "God's teaching about marriage shows us that such a serious step requires maturity and preparation."

Thank God for church, school, Christian friends, and any other positive influences on our young people. But the final source of understanding and security—and God's original plan— is still a close relationship between a teen-ager and his parents in the Christian family.

SCRIPTURE FOR STUDY

Deut. 7:1-6	Dan. 1
Ps. 119:9-11	Luke 9:23, 57-62
Eccles. 12:1-7; 13-14	John 15:18-27

QUESTIONS FOR DISCUSSION

1. Could the loneliness described by the teenager who ran away ever happen in a Christian home? Under what circumstances?

2. How flexible can Christian parents be in recognizing the different values and interests of their teen-agers?
3. How long is a teen-ager bound by Scripture to obey his parents and how can this obedience be enforced?
4. In what ways can Christian parents *show* love and acceptance to their teen-agers?
5. What other issues would you list as representing conflict between a Christian teen-ager's beliefs and what the world is telling him? What are some biblical answers to these conflicts?

SECTION
TWO
Important Issues

8
Family
Worship

Bill and Sue Langley are determined to be effective Christian parents. Each day they gather their three children around the table after supper for a half hour of family worship. The time is spent in Bible reading, prayer, and an occasional song.

Sounds good, doesn't it? But all is not well at the Langley family devotions. Greg (15) resents missing his favorite television program. Cindy (12) complains that she can't spare the time from homework responsibilities. Steve (7) is uninterested and shows it by making noises and disturbing the others. The more the children fuss, the more Bill and Sue force the issue. Some evenings family worship erupts in a verbal battle upsetting everyone for the next several hours!

Where have the Langleys gone wrong? Rather than answering that question directly, let's take a look at some of the issues involved in effective family worship. Then perhaps the problems at the Langley house will become more obvious and you can pinpoint the kind of solutions that will help.

Biblical Foundations

Some people think that the Bible contains many passages on the importance and technique of family worship. Actually it does not. But the general tone of both Old and New Testaments certainly implies that the home is the central source of spiritual teaching in God's plan. One key passage is Deuteronomy 6:4-9:

> O Israel, listen: Jehovah is our God, Jehovah alone. You must love him with all your heart, soul, and might. And you must think constantly about these commandments I am giving you today. You must teach them to your children and talk about them when you are at home or out for a walk; at bedtime and the first thing in the morning. Tie them on your finger, wear them on your forehead, and write them on the doorposts of your house!" (TLB).

The Jewish leaders in the later history of the nation began to follow such commands literally by tying boxes to their foreheads and left arms. The small containers, called phylacteries, held tiny scrolls with four passages from the Old Testament (including the one above). It was this kind of rigid legalism that Jesus condemned in the Pharisees.

Surely the passage is symbolical. Moses might

have said, "The things of the Lord should fill your homes at all times. Be free to talk about spiritual things with your children just as normally as you would discuss anything else."

It is possible to make the same mistake of wooden ritualism with family worship. Spiritual times with our children should never become a sterile practice of "tying boxes on foreheads and wrists."

General Principles

It may be important to notice that the Bible does *not* dictate any procedures for family worship. Each Christian family is free to define for itself how the practice of devotions can best be carried out in their home. Here are three principles which many Christian parents have found helpful:

Flexibility: Try to avoid a strict authoritarianism in such matters as time, format, and style of the family worship time. Mottos like "No Bible—No Breakfast" are catchy and may have some value in self-discipline but severe restrictions may hinder rather than help to achieve productivity in family life. Many families find that the morning rush just would not tolerate additional activities.

Practicality: Family worship should be fitted to the children's interests and needs. High level discussions of theological issues are good for husbands and wives but can be deadly at family devotions.

61

Naturalness: As Deuteronomy 6 implies, "don't make a big deal" out of family worship time. It should be a usual and expected pattern in the home. Too much fanfare makes it appear to be an abnormal part of Christian family life. Every time Bill Langley forces the issue, he may be building resistance in his teen-agers.

Practical Guidelines

Most Christian parents vote in favor of family worship. Their constant questions reflect more on the "how" than the "why." To enforce patterns which have worked for some families as a format to be adopted by others may not be a good plan. Some general guidelines may be helpful. What do you think of these?

Variation: G. Weatherly writes, "Interest will be retained as parents keep their family devotions from becoming a meaningless routine of doing the same thing in the same way at the same time each day. Planned variety can prevent this from happening" (*Sunday School Times and Gospel Herald,* Dec. 1, 1972, p. 22). We agree. Attention spans of small children require multiple and differing activities and adults like variety too.

Participation: Family worship should not be a time when dad plays pastor. Most children enjoy getting into the act and will enthusiastically do what they are asked to do. Devotions then involve the total family.

Delegation: We have found it productive to

carry participation one step further. Each member of the family is in charge of family worship one night of the week. The leader may have any kind of a program he or she wishes. In our family the most creative devotional leader is the youngest child who has on various occasions prepared role-playing sequences, home-made visuals for stories, special music, offerings, and even once conducted a family communion service!

Habituation: Families get into habits just as individuals do. Sometimes the habits are not helpful—like missing church everytime we have Sunday company. But family worship should become a habit that draws family members together and makes each one feel he is contributing to, as well as drawing on, the family's spiritual resources.

Common Errors

Family worship usually turns sour when we fall into one or more of the following traps. Check each one in conjunction with Bill Langley's problems—and perhaps, your own.

- Beginning too late: Family worship should be a life-style for children from the earliest possible age.
- Inadequate materials: Adult devotional booklets and difficult Bible translations don't help the cause.
- Forced involvement: Pressure to conform is not always good—especially with teenagers.

- Rigid adherence: Don't let guilt clouds hang over the family when devotions are missed once in a while.
- Carelessness: Lack of planning, frequent forgetting, irrelevance, all tend to deteriorate the importance of family worship.

SCRIPTURE FOR STUDY

Deut. 6:4-9, 20-25   Eph. 6:4
Zech. 7   II Tim. 3:14-17

QUESTIONS FOR DISCUSSION

1. Is prayer before meals a form of family worship? Should it be? Can it be?
2. How soon are young children able to participate in family worship? What can we do about their short attention span?
3. Think of some ways children of various ages can be involved in family worship.
4. If a family has not conducted group devotions until the children are teen-agers, how can they successfully start at that point?
5. List at least ten different activities that could be a part of effective family worship.

9
Common Problems in Child-Parent Relationships

All parents will probably face one or more of the following problems while in the process of raising their children. But a family relationship which is saturated with love will find the solutions to the problems much more quickly than a family in which little or no love is shown.

Some authorities suggest that it is more important for children to know that their parents love each other than it is for children to know that they themselves are loved. They may have a good point.

On the other hand, an article by Jeannette Acrea in *Psychology for Living* (June 1972) tells of a girl named Judy who was hurt very deeply and eventually needed psychotherapy because her mother and father loved each other so much that they found very little time for her. She felt left out, unimportant, and unnoticed.

It is good for children to see their parents express love for each other but children must also be held, hugged, kissed, and told of the parents' love for them.

There are other ways of showing love besides physical contact. We show love by playing and doing things with our children. We also show love by talking, reading, or just sitting quietly together.

Timidity and Fear

Mary is a shy and fearful child, afraid of any new situations. Her fear involves the dark, storms, and animals. Often she wants to sleep with her parents or cries uncontrollably. Although her parents may not understand and try to reason with her, talking probably will not change the situation.

Not all fear is bad. Because there are certain things such as fire, deep water, or a busy street which can hurt a child, we must teach him to have a certain amount of fear. The problem is that some parents instill unwarranted fear into a child unknowingly, either by their own phobias or by their actions and comments.

Fear is a learned emotion. A child accumulates fear from contact with other people. Consequently, we can also teach him *not* to have fear. In the book, *Living with Children* by

Patterson and Gullion, there are several good suggestions offered for dealing with the frightened child. One suggestion is training a child to decrease his fear by positive reinforcers.

Let's consider Mary's fear of animals. We can teach Mary that the proper gentle treatment of the kitty reduces the need to be afraid. When the kitty is brought into the room, if Mary remains calm and yet observes from a distance without becoming frightened and crying, we reward that behavior by praise and perhaps a piece of candy. But if Mary begins to scream, the worst thing the mother can do is to take the child into her arms to comfort her because that is reinforcing the very opposite behavior of what we are trying to accomplish. Gradually the child might be able to touch the kitty and later hold the kitty. Don't force such behavior too quickly and reward each level of achievement with praise.

This principle can be applied to almost any difficult situation the shy, fearful child may be facing and can be a great help in teaching him self-confidence and courage. One does not have to subscribe to the basic premises of behavioristic psychology to utilize its principles of positive reinforcement.

The loving Christian parent can also give strength to his child from the Word of God. The child can begin to understand the depth of God's love and promises such as "There is no fear in love; but perfect love casteth out fear:

because fear hath torment. He that feareth is not made perfect in love" (I John 4:18). Then soon we will begin to see victory over fear.

Hyperactivity

Perhaps you've been thinking that "shy, retiring, and fearful" certainly does not describe your children. Noisy, loud, and full of exuberance would be more like it. Maybe there never seems to be enough peace and quiet around the house.

All children are active in varying degrees just because they are children. Parents must allow for a certain amount of rough and tumble play. The key to the situation is that children learn the proper place and time for boisterous play. Parents help the situation by always being consistent. If they say that the yard and the family room are the only places for rough play but do not carry through with enforcement, then the children soon revert to loud, noisy running through the house, and the battle is on.

Agree on a punishment when the rule is broken and a reward when the rule is remembered. Then carry out the plan. Hyperactivity might have a neurological cause and a medical examination is usually a wise investment.

Rebellion

There can be situations where a child becomes so extremely aggressive, destructive, or rebellious that professional help is needed. These things can be the symptoms of a deeper problem and the parents should act accordingly to help the child find the answers to his anxieties.

There are other problems that parents often have with their children which could come under the general category of specific sins. The Bible speaks out very strongly about such things as lying, stealing, anger and jealousy. In Ephesians 4:25-28 we read,

> Stop lying to each other; tell the truth, for we are parts of each other and when we lie to each other we are hurting ourselves. If you are angry, don't sin by nursing your grudge. Don't let the sun go down with you still angry—get over it quickly; for when you are angry you give a mighty foothold to the devil. If anyone is stealing he must stop it and begin using those hands of his for honest work so he can give to others in need (TLB).

The child who consistently lies, steals, or has outbursts of anger must be made to realize the seriousness of his behavior, not only in the eyes of his parents, but also in the eyes of God.

Because God knew that children are born with a sinful nature and they would find it much easier to sin than to do what pleases God, He gave them parents. Then He told those parents what to do:

> The rod and reproof give wisdom: but a child left to himself bringeth his mother to

shame. ... Correct thy son, and he shall
give thee rest; yea, he shall give delight
unto thy soul (Prov. 29:15-17).

There are no easy, glib answers to any of the
behavioral problems we have with our children.
But Christian parents can claim the guidance and
instruction of the Holy Spirit. As we allow Him
to control our lives, He will lead us into all
truth.

SCRIPTURE FOR STUDY

Ps. 51:5   Eph. 4:25-28
Prov. 29:15-17   I Tim. 5:4
John 4:18   I John 1:8-10

QUESTIONS FOR DISCUSSION

1. Identify several ways in which parents can
   show love to their children.
2. What does the Bible say about the sin nature
   of children?
3. How does chronic hyperactivity demonstrate
   itself in a child's behavior?
4. How do parents transfer their own fears and
   prejudices to children? Is there a way to minimize this negative transfer?
5. How can consistent and cooperative child-care
   take place if one parent is not a Christian?

10
The Family
that
Plays Together

A recent newspaper headline blared the warning, "Family Disaster Feared." The writer was quoting psychiatrist Graham B. Blaine, Jr. of the Harvard Medical Services. Blaine suggests that there is growing alienation between children and their parents. Neurotic illness, serious drug abuse, and delinquency also seem to be related to faulty family relationships. His proposal is to restructure family life so that, beginning with babyhood through age seventeen, the child would be placed in the care of others from eight in the morning till six in the evening, six days a week, eleven months of the year!

Perhaps your first reaction is to think that such a suggestion is ridiculous and parents will never agree to do such a thing. But parents are coming very close to Blaine's idea right now. They become obsessed with jobs, clubs and, even church activities, so that there remains little time for family togetherness.

A friend commented to us not long ago that her memories of home were rather negative. Her father taught at a Christian college and he never had time to be home. Each evening held a committee meeting, a speaking engagement, or some other responsibility.

Christian parents need to learn to live with, not in spite of, or even for, their children. Family togetherness needs to be planned and not just allowed to happen.

Play at Home

Let us consider some of the things to do right at home, especially during the long winter evenings. One most enriching pastime is reading. When the children are small, good books can be read to them. As they get older they may want to read books of their own interest and reading level. The daily newspaper, weekly Sunday School papers, *National Geographic,* children's classics such as *Heidi, Black Beauty,* or Kipling's stories make for interesting and exciting reading.

Scrapbooks can be a fine family project. Try a picture scrapbook of family outings and events. Or perhaps on a specific subject such as animals, insects, birds, a foreign country or just the protection of special school items such as poems or stories written by the children. Our daughter had great fun preparing a scrapbook which visualized songs.

Children love to play and perhaps none of us ever outgrow the need for games. Family activities can include table games, puzzles, quizzes, and ping pong.

Hobbies such as collecting coins, stamps, shells, or rocks can be interesting, educational, and will fill many long hours. Some hobbies (painting, woodworking, sewing, or photography) can be carried on all through the adult years.

We dare not ignore television since it is perhaps the biggest user of family time. Perhaps this is not entirely bad because television programming has a great deal of good information and entertainment to offer our children. Much has been written about how television is affecting our children. One thing is sure, Christian parents must not ignore their responsibility to control, censor, and guide the children in choosing their programs. Not even all so-called "children's programs" may be acceptable to Christian parents.

The primary danger of television lies in the likelihood that it will monopolize our time and crowd out many of the other adventures we could be having with our children.

In the Yard

What about the outdoors? The possibilities are unlimited. There is sledding, ice skating, tobogganing, touch football, catch, tag, basketball, and other games. The yard can become a ball field, a badminton court, or a place for croquet, lawn darts, or just catching fire-flies after dark.

Short Trips

Summer also gives opportunities for picnics to a nearby park, a bicycle ride, or a weekend camping trip. Camping has become a quite popular way of taking a family vacation and is a wonderful way of bringing a family close together. Setting up the campsite, finding wood, building a fire, and cooking the food become a family project.

Many of these outside activities can give dad wonderful teaching opportunities. Not only will he be able to teach various skills, but also Christian character, attitudes, and good sportsmanship. He might serve as coach or referee for a neighborhood game. Doing things like this with our children means a great deal to them.

Traveling with Children

Summer usually brings vacation time. As teen-agers look back on their childhood, some of the happiest memories are often related to family vacations and holidays.

Vacations should be planned and eagerly anticipated by the entire family. Perhaps the place is chosen on the basis of economics. By saving early, family vacations can be a reality without going into debt for the next six months.

A vacation does not have to be long, far away, or expensive to be a happy and positive family experience.

One family decided one year to see their own city just as though they were visitors. They visited all the parks, museums, the zoo, etc. It was fun becoming better acquainted with the city and yet finding many new and interesting things.

After the location has been decided and you've started to save the needed money, start gathering interesting things for the children to do in the car. There is nothing more hectic than to have several fighting children crammed in a car with two irritated and tired parents. Take along car games, books, and plenty of ideas for passing the hours in a happy sharing time. Keeping a diary, making a scrapbook, taking pictures, and reading travel guides will add pleasure and value to the trip.

Special Occasions

Birthdays and major holidays should be times when happy memories and even family traditions are formed. These experiences need not become ritualistic, but children feel security in the family setting of knowing that every Christmas things will happen in somewhat the same pattern. Alma Jones in "Fun with Children" suggests

Scientific studies show that maladjustments of children decrease as family recreation increases; also that understanding and confidence between parents and children increase as shared activities and good times increase (The American Institute of Family Relations, Pub. No. 226).

Does all of this sound too idealistic? Is it impossible with our busy schedules? With God's help, it is not only possible, but necessary and our children and their futures are worth the effort.

SCRIPTURE FOR STUDY

Lev. 23:33-44   Ps. 37:4-5
Ps. 16:11   I Cor. 10:31

QUESTIONS FOR DISCUSSION

1. Is there any Biblical evidence that parents should provide leisure time leadership for their children?
2. How high a priority should vacations have in the family budget?
3. Think of creative possibilities for family togetherness other than those mentioned by the authors.
4. Discuss Blaine's proposal for enforced day care programs.
5. Discuss the relationship between *quantity* and *quality* of leisure time spent with children.

11
The
Missing
Dimension

An overwhelming percent of your child's time is spent under the influence of three social groups: the home, the church, and the school. Out of approximately one hundred waking hours in a week, a Christian child will spend thirty-five to forty in school, five or six in church and related ministries, and almost all the rest at home. Compulsory education demands a portion of your child's time, almost equal to half his waking hours each week! And you have no voice in the teachers, curriculum, rules, or goals of the school. Unless, of course, you are among the growing number of parents who send their children to Christian schools.

Think of these three influences as the triangle of a child's life.

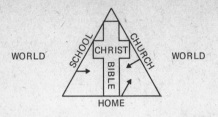

When all three agree on truth and values, a wholistic consistency assists parents in their task of raising godly children. All the pieces fit and the child can "get it all together" with a minimum of frustration and turmoil.

But when one of the sides of the triangle presents an opposing and contradictory emphasis, the other two must compensate. Time which could have been spent on constructive edification must be channeled into defensive teaching and counter-action.

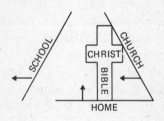

Philosophical Considerations

If all truth is God's truth (and it is), then a system of truth-seeking which omits or denies God is engaging in futile efforts to create its own truth. In the final analysis all sources of truth can be lumped into two categories: *Revelationism* or *Rationalism*.

Revelationism Says . .	*Rationalism Says . . .*
There is a God	There is only man
Man was created in God's image	Man evolved into a thinking animal
God is self-revealed in the Bible	The Bible is literature, composed of myth and ancient error
A child is sinful and needs to have his heart changed by God	A child is only bad because of his negative environment
God can work supernaturally in His world and in His people	All phenomena must have natural explanations
True values point to spiritual and eternal things	Values change in a shifting society—it's all relative
Christian teacher and student are both guided by the Holy Spirit	The best learning is reinforced conditioning in a controlled environment
Morality and behavior have absolute guidelines in Scripture	There are no absolute "rights and wrongs"—society's standards are constantly changing

Biblical Examples

The Bible makes it very plain that believers in both Old and New Testaments considered home the primary place for godly teaching and training. We have already referred to Deuteronomy 6 several times in these few chapters. Separation is an unpopular but quite biblical concept even though it is sometimes overdone by some Christians. Check again God's warning to Israel just before they moved in to take over Canaan (Deut. 7:1-11).

After the return from exile, synagogue schools became the popular instructional system of the Jews. We see in Timothy's case, however, that even these elaborate educational institutions did not replace but rather supplemented religious teaching in the home (II Tim. 1:3-5; 3:14-15).

How about the early Christians? Did they send their children to public schools? Most certainly not! Not because the Roman P.S. 22 was too expensive, or because they were not permitted to use the system. They recognized that the values and morals of pagan education were diametrically opposed to the teachings of Jesus Christ. Until the church established its own schools in the third century, Christian parents taught their children at home.

Social Concerns

One of the practical benefits of a Christian school is the atmosphere in which a child learns. The hours of potential influence are not limited to the actual classroom sessions. Recess, lunch time, social life, and athletics all provide inputs for molding a life. The Christian school offers some obvious advantages:

1. A parental voice in guiding the affairs of the school. Parochial (church-control) organization offers less opportunity for influence than parent-society (independent board) organization, but either should allow parents to have a voice in school affairs. Indeed, this is one of the major distinctions of a private school and Christian parents should make every effort to make their voices heard in institutional policy.

2. An emphasis on patriotism. Love and respect for God and country are the missing ingredients in most public schools in our day. One does not have to equate evangelicalism with conservative politics to believe that sincere Christians should take Romans 13:1-7 seriously.

3. An opportunity to meet, play with, date, and develop friendships with other Christians.

4. Minimal difficulty with drugs and abusive language.

5. The opportunity for parent and teacher to become a team—praying for, counseling, and guiding the intellectual and spiritual growth of the child.

Common Objections

Some of our readers have already reacted negatively to the emphasis of this chapter. But remember, we are speaking educationally as teachers, not only from the emotional parental viewpoint. Not all Christian schools meet satisfactory standards just as all public schools do not. But we believe the case can be defended biblically, philosophically, and practically. Just quickly, let's look at some hesitation people have concerning Christian schools:

"The teachers aren't well trained." In most cases, this objection is a myth. What *is* proper preparation for a Christian teacher? Do secular state boards of education have satisfactory standards? There is a difference between being certified and being qualified.

"The Christian school is a hothouse—an unnatural hideaway from reality." In a sense, it should be. Young children need to be protected from the sin and violence of our barbarian culture. Besides, where do we find a text that says that the primary task of school children is evangelism? And for that role, there are ample hours away from school in the all-too-natural neighborhood environment.

"Christians shouldn't abandon the public schools." Right! And there is hardly any danger that they will. Some Christian teachers will continue to be called to render whatever witness they can, although opportunities are decreasing year by year. And the fear that all Christian parents will send their children to Christian schools is about as valid as the fear expressed by the lady who once asked, "What will we do if all of our young people should go to the mission field?"

Many Christian parents, because of their beliefs, geographical location, or lack of finances, will not send their children to Christian schools. But through sacrifice, and perhaps, pioneering in efforts to start a school, many should consider the possibility and weigh the values of strengthening that third leg of the triangle.

SCRIPTURE FOR STUDY

Deut. 7:1-11   Col. 2:2-8
Rom. 13:1-7   II Tim. 1:3-5
Eph. 4:17-24   II Tim. 3:14-17

QUESTIONS FOR DISCUSSION

1. Name and discuss some ideas children will learn in public education which are contrary to what we might teach them at home.
2. What evidence is there that compulsory public education has preempted the natural rights of parents?
3. Discuss the statement, "Too many Christian parents have given over by default the training of their children to the church and public school."
4. Do you agree with the authors that secular education is almost exclusively "rationalistic"? What difference does it make?
5. How can parents whose children attend public schools obtain a greater voice in school affairs?

12
Recycling the Process

In the system of the human race, the reproduction of children almost always leads to the reproduction of parents. We also know that the atmosphere of a child's home determines, to a significant degree, the kind of parent he will ultimately become. There is a subconscious pattern development which creates a basis for parental behavior—either positive or negative.

It is not true that an alert young adult whose home background has been anything but biblical is therefore locked into that pattern. By careful planning, self-adjustment, and a generous measure of the grace of God, such a person could become a very effective parent. But we should think in the other direction. If we really want to operate and then reproduce Christian homes, how can we as parents aim toward a positive recycling process?

We have already indicated that parents' behavior and attitudes in the home are experience-molding from the earliest years. But since we cannot discuss the whole process, let's focus on the late teen years with the understanding that many of these things will have been going on, almost since birth. How can we help our teen-agers prepare for Christian family relations?

Teach Them What Christian Marriage Is

You can see that this little book has now come full cycle. In the first chapter we talked about what a newly married couple should do to set a home atmosphere for their yet unborn children. Now it's twenty years later and those children are about to become parents.

While recognizing that our own husband-wife and parent-child relations have been the most dominant influence, we should also deliberately plan to verbally teach our teen-agers what they need to know about marriage. Three aspects seem to rise to the fore:

1. The purpose of Christian marriage
2. Biblical roles for family members and how to carry these out
3. What problems and joys to expect and how to cope with them

Some will say that these things can't be taught but must be experienced. Others will complain that telling young people too much before marriage will take away the joy of discovery.

But our problem surely has never been that we teach our children too much! And the fact remains that marriage is still the most important social and spiritual dimension of life, yet it is the one which thousands enter ill-equipped and poorly prepared.

Show Them a Biblical Model

Nick Thompson is a Christian young man who just recently passed his eighteenth birthday. On the surface he appears to be serious, spiritually-minded and quite mature. But Nick himself knows he is a troubled boy. His family has always been closely connected to the church and both parents have held offices. The pastor and most of the other members think of the Thompsons as an ideal family. But Nick knows the inside story.

He has recently had reason to doubt dad's love for mom. Of course, there is no overt infidelity and even very little arguing. But the positive side of the ledger is empty. Nick has not seen his dad openly express love to his mom either verbally or physically. He's trying hard to assume that it's there, but this atmosphere of sterility has given Nick a hang-up about showing affection to anyone else.

Not only that, but since he has been old enough to discuss family matters with his parents, he has discovered that Mr. Thompson tries to "adjust" figures on his income tax return, asks friends downtown to "fix" an occasional parking ticket, and speaks critically and unkindly about other church members when they disagree with his views.

Nick and dad had a major blow-up last week over pot. Although he has no desire to smoke marijuana himself, Nick defended legalization just on principle. Dad almost choked on his cigarette while denouncing anyone who would use drugs in any form.

Nick's problem, of course, is a credibility gap. Should he design a life-style like the one his parents tell him about or like the one they live? In the crucial years immediately preceding his own marriage Nick is watching a negative demonstration of biblical roles, behavior, and ethics in his own home.

Warn Them about the Pitfalls

And expect in advance that such "warning" will often be equated with "nagging." When you think about it, Jeremiah and Ezekiel were considered "nags" by those to whom they ministered. There are at least six danger zones in dating, engagement, and marriage that should be clearly marked by parents who care:

1. Masturbation
2. Emotional confusion of "going steady"
3. Lust and evil thoughts
4. Premarital sex
5. Missing or not caring about God's will
6. Premature marriage

Each of these danger zones has an alternative on the positive and Biblical side.

1. Masturbation is a selfish practice that begins with impure thoughts and ends in uncontrollable habits. God's answer is *His ownership of both mind and body* (I Cor. 6:9-20; Col. 3:1-14).

2. The emotional conflict of going steady can be countered with a casual, diversified dating life which sees Christians of the opposite sex as genuine friends and not always potential partners for sex or marriage (Prov. 18:24; John 15:15).

3. Lust and evil thoughts are sin. We dare not excuse them nor can we afford to feed them with erotic magazines and books (I Tim. 1:7; Phil. 4:8-9; II Tim. 2:22).

4. Premarital sex is sin because God has ordained that sexual relations are to be confined within the marriage bond (I Cor. 7:1-5; Heb. 13:4).

5. Missing God's will does not automatically produce a life of misery and unhappiness but our teens need to know how to consider God's choice of a marriage partner (John 7:17; Rom. 12:1, 2).

6. Premature marriage militates against the high-level, careful planning God wants His children to give to marriage and family (Eph. 5:15-33).

The local church should also assist parents in helping Christian teens prepare for marriage. Classes, youth programs, sex education, and counseling are supportive of what parents are doing in the home to "show and tell" what Christian marriage is all about.

SCRIPTURE FOR STUDY

Prov. 22:6	I Cor. 7:1-5
John 7:17	Eph. 5:15-33
Phil. 4:8, 9	I Tim. 1:7
Col. 3:1-14	II Tim. 1:3-6
Rom. 12:1, 2	II Tim. 2:22
I Cor. 6:9-20	Heb. 13:4

QUESTIONS FOR DISCUSSION

1. What can we do to help teens, whose homes are broken, overcome the effects of that negative experience?
2. Name some arguments both for and against teen-agers going steady.
3. How much influence should Christian parents exert over their young people's choice of dating and marriage partners?
4. The chapter suggests that Christian parents should prepare teen-agers for the problems and joys of marriage. What are some of those problems and joys?
5. Do you agree that most Christian teen-age girls are not aware of the explosive potential of the way they dress and act? How can parents handle this difficult problem?